D1706840

EDDIE BAUER
DOWN JACKET DEVELOPER

REBECCA FELIX

Checkerboard Library
An Imprint of Abdo Publishing
abdopublishing.com

ABDOPUBLISHING.COM

Published by Abdo Publishing, a division of ABDO, PO Box 398166, Minneapolis, Minnesota 55439.

Checkerboard Library™ is a trademark and logo of Abdo Publishing.

Printed in the United States of America, North Mankato, Minnesota
062017
092017

Design: Emily O'Malley, Mighty Media, Inc.
Production: Emily O'Malley, Mighty Media, Inc.
Series Editor: Katherine Hengel Frankowski
Cover Photographs: Courtesy of the Eddie Bauer Archives (left); Shutterstock (right)
Interior Photographs: AP Images, p. 27; Courtesy of the Eddie Bauer Archives, pp. 9, 11, 13, 15, 19, 21; iStockphoto, pp. 5, 17; Shutterstock, pp. 7, 22 (bottom), 23 (top), 23 (middle), 23 (bottom), 25; Wikimedia Commons, p. 22 (top)

Publisher's Cataloging-in-Publication Data

Names: Felix, Rebecca, author.
Title: Eddie Bauer: down jacket developer / by Rebecca Felix.
Other titles: Down jacket developer
Description: Minneapolis, MN : Abdo Publishing, 2018. | Series: First in fashion | Includes bibliographical references and index.
Identifiers: LCCN 2016962500 | ISBN 9781532110733 (lib. bdg.) | ISBN 9781680788587 (ebook)
Subjects: LCSH: Bauer, Eddie, 1899-1986--Juvenile literature. | Fashion designer--United States--Biography--Juvenile literature. | Sporting goods industry--United States--Biography--Juvenile literature. | Camping equipment industry--United States--Biography--Juvenile literature. | Sports clothes industry--United States--Biography--Juvenile literature.
Classification: DDC 746.9 [B]--dc23
LC record available at http://lccn.loc.gov/2016962500

CONTENTS

SUCCESSFUL SPORTSMAN

It's Saturday afternoon, and you're going sledding. You zip up your **down** jacket and head outside. The icy air may be cold on your face. But your body stays warm and toasty. This is the power of down!

Outdoorsman Eddie Bauer created the first down jackets in North America. The jackets were very lightweight and warm. They were popular with mountain climbers, skiers, and hunters.

Bauer designed other cold-weather garments too. He also made sporting goods. Every item he sold was tested in rugged conditions. Bauer's products were made to handle extreme weather and wear.

Bauer's commitment to quality made him famous. Today, there are more than 600 Eddie Bauer stores all over the world. The company also sells goods through catalogs and online. But Eddie Bauer's story began in the forests of Washington State.

There is at least one Eddie Bauer store in all 50 US states!

OUTDOORSY UPBRINGING

Eddie Bauer was born on October 19, 1899, in Orcas Island, Washington. His parents were Jacob and Marie Bauer. Jacob and Marie were farmers. Eddie had six brothers and sisters. The Bauer family lived in a log cabin.

Eddie's father hunted the island's forests and fished its coasts. He passed his love of the outdoors on to his son. He taught Eddie everything he knew about hunting and fishing.

In 1904, the Bauers left their farm. They moved to the town of Yarrow Point, Washington. Five years later, at age ten, Eddie got a job in nearby Seattle. He worked as a **caddie** at Seattle Golf Club.

In 1913, Eddie's parents separated. Young Eddie moved to Seattle with his mother. He was in eighth grade at the time. He dropped out of school to focus on work. He took a job at a sporting goods store called Piper & Taft. It was a job that would shape his entire future.

Orcas Island is part of the San Juan chain of islands in the Pacific Ocean.

MOVING UP

Eddie worked hard at his new job at Piper & Taft. He ran errands, stocked shelves, and washed windows. Eddie also learned many new skills. For example, he learned to make fishing poles and lures. He learned to repair tennis **rackets** and golf clubs. He also learned a lot about running a business.

After four years, Eddie's bosses promoted him. He was no longer washing windows! Instead, he was in charge of product displays. Eddie was responsible for arranging the store's products in an appealing way.

Eddie was very familiar with the products he sold. As a hunter and fisherman, he used them all the time. So, Eddie decided to show customers what the products could do. He created store displays that included the big fish he had caught.

Bauer had loved dogs since his youth and brought his dogs to help him hunt.

Eddie's displays attracted customers and increased sales. The displays also made Eddie famous. Soon, he was known around Seattle as a skilled fisherman.

BAUER'S BUSINESSES

Bauer kept improving his sportsman's skills. He also kept learning about sporting goods. He left Piper & Taft in about 1919. He opened his own sporting goods business in Seattle. It was called Eddie Bauer's Tennis Shop.

Bauer's shop focused on repairing high-quality tennis **rackets** for local players. Bauer closed his store during the fall and winter. He used that time to go camping, fishing, and hunting.

Soon, Bauer expanded his store's offerings. He began selling golf clubs, fishing tackle, and other sporting goods. In 1920, Bauer closed his tennis shop and opened a new, larger store. It was called Eddie Bauer's Sport Shop.

THE EDDIE BAUER CREED

In 1922, Bauer wrote the Eddie Bauer **Creed**. The creed explains his commitment to quality, value, and service. The creed still guides the company today.

Like Bauer's first shop, the new one sold sporting goods. Bauer gave every customer a **guarantee**. The guarantee promised customers that Bauer's products were high quality. This promise became the heart of his company and brand.

Bauer opened Eddie Bauer's Sport Shop with $10,000 profit from his previous store and a matching bank loan.

GAME, SET, MATCH

Each year, Bauer's company grew. But he was not always successful in love. In the early 1920s, Bauer got married. Little is known about this marriage. Shortly after they were married, the couple divorced.

Nearly a decade later, Bauer met Christine Heltborg while he was out testing equipment. The two shared a love of outdoor sports. They married on February 21, 1929. Their son, Eddie Jr., was born on February 5, 1938.

Bauer kept growing his business and exploring his passions. He started mountain climbing and saltwater fishing. He also started playing a new sport called badminton.

In badminton, players use **rackets** to hit a **shuttlecock** across a high net. Bauer realized that the shuttlecock's weight and shape mattered. He began designing new, improved shuttlecocks.

Bauer and Christine Heltborg shared many outdoor interests, including skiing in the Washington mountains. Bauer called his wife his "wilderness companion."

In 1934, Bauer patented his new **shuttlecock** design. It quickly became the standard in badminton. In fact, it still is today! Soon, another Bauer invention would change the sporting world.

HARROWING HIKE

Bauer was an inventor. Nearly everything he did gave him ideas! He was always testing equipment on outdoor adventures. Often, these trials inspired him to invent new products. In fact, a near-death experience resulted in his most famous creation.

In January 1935, Bauer and his friend Red Carlson went fishing. It was winter on the **Olympic Peninsula**. The men caught a lot of fish early in the day. Then they began the hike back to their car. Each man carried his gear and a large bag of fish on his back.

Both men were wearing wool shirts and jackets. As they hiked, the outdoor temperature began to rise. The heat plus their heavy loads caused them to sweat. The sweat and water from the wet bags of fish soaked their jackets. The jackets became very heavy and wet.

Later in the day, the outdoor temperature dropped. Bauer's wet garments froze. He became very tired

Bauer didn't let his near-death experience impact his love of the outdoors. He remained an accomplished fisherman for his whole life.

and fell behind. Soon, Bauer felt the **symptoms** of **hypothermia**. He knew he had to increase his body temperature quickly. If he didn't, he would die.

FASHION FACTOID

Inuit people made waterproof jackets out of the intestines of walruses and seals.

Carlson was too far ahead to hear Bauer's calls for help. Luckily, Bauer was carrying a gun. He shot two **rounds** into the air to alert Carlson. Carlson found Bauer and helped him to safety.

DOWN IDEA

Bauer was grateful to have survived. But his experience got him thinking. He wished he'd had a better jacket that day. He wanted a jacket that was warm but light. He also wanted air to **circulate** throughout the jacket.

Bauer started thinking about how to improve cold-weather jackets. He recalled his uncle's war stories. Bauer's uncle had spent time in the Russian army. He said the Russian officers often wore coats stuffed with feathers. The feathers were light but very warm. Bauer decided to create a feather jacket of his own.

Bauer got right to work. He already knew several feather suppliers. They sold him feathers for certain

The soft feathers underneath a goose's outer feathers are called down. These feathers are used in bedding, pillows, sleeping bags, and more to keep people comfortable and warm.

fishing lures. These same suppliers provided Bauer with quality goose **down** for his new jacket.

Next, Bauer hired a **seamstress** to make a model. The model was made using breathable cotton. The seamstress stitched diamond shapes into the cotton. This evenly trapped the feathers in place. The next step was to put the jacket to the test.

FEATHER FRENZY

Bauer took his new jacket to his friend Ome Daiber. Daiber was a skilled mountain climber. He was very excited about Bauer's new jacket! Daiber felt that Bauer's jacket could change the climbing world.

Daiber owned a manufacturing business. So, he helped Bauer produce more jackets to sell. They called them Eddie Bauer Blizzard-Proof Jackets. Meanwhile, Bauer continued to improve the garment. In 1936, Bauer renamed it the Skyliner.

Bauer began advertising the Skyliner in outdoor magazines. Many readers already wanted goose **down**

LABRADOR LOVE

In 1930, Bauer heard about a black Labrador retriever named Blackie. His friends told him Blackie was an amazing hunter. So, Bauer drove to Canada and bought her. Blackie was Bauer's beloved hunting partner for many years. In retirement, Bauer bred black Labs for hunting.

The Skyliner's slogan was "Lighter than a feather, warmer than ten sweaters."

jackets. But they didn't know where to buy them. Thanks to Bauer's ads, now they did! Orders started coming in right away. And Bauer's small store got very, very busy.

SOLDIERS & SALES

In the coming years, Skyliner sales rose. In 1940, Bauer patented the Skyliner jacket. He also started labeling each one to build his brand. The labels said "Eddie Bauer, Seattle, U.S.A."

In 1942, Bauer's business changed. The United States had just entered **World War II**. To help with the war effort, the US government asked businesses to make war goods. So, Bauer began making products for soldiers instead of sportsmen.

For soldiers, Bauer made **down** sleeping bags. He also made down flight suits for pilots. These suits kept pilots warm. They could also float, in case the pilots landed in water. And, each had the Eddie Bauer label.

When the war ended, soldiers remembered Bauer's gear. It had kept them warm, dry, and safe. Many sent Bauer thank-you letters. They all wanted to know where they could buy Eddie Bauer products.

Airmen stationed in Alaska during World War II loved Eddie Bauer products. They even bet the brand's sleeping bags and jackets in card games!

Bauer knew it was time to make his products available beyond Seattle. So, in 1945, he released the company's first catalog. It was mailed around the country. US servicemen were among Eddie Bauer's top buyers that year.

FASHION TIME MACHINE

COTE, 400s–1600s **Medieval** men wore jackets called cotes. They had long sleeves, fitted waists, and buttons up the front.

VARSITY JACKET, 1930s In the 1930s, US high schools and colleges created varsity jackets. These wool jackets had leather sleeves. Students placed school activity patches on the sleeves. Varsity jackets are still worn today.

DOWN JACKET, 1940s Many **cultures** have used **down** for warmth throughout history. But Bauer made down jackets popular in the 1940s. Today, these cozy coats are often called puffer jackets. They come in many different colors and lengths.

BIKER JACKET, 1950s Biker jackets are short, fitted leather jackets. They have zippers running up the front. They were first worn in the United States by motorcyclists in the late 1940s. By the 1950s, nearly everyone was wearing them!

PARKA, 1960s **Parkas** are loose-fitting, long jackets with fur-lined hoods. In the 1960s, parkas became trendy in Europe. But they date back to ancient times. Many modern parkas are a combination of a traditional parka and a down jacket.

A NEW GENERATION

Bauer's catalog helped his business grow. But fulfilling catalog orders was a lot of work. Plus, Bauer was tired. Making thousands of war items had worn him out. By 1949, Bauer knew he needed help.

Bauer asked his friend William Niemi for support. Niemi was an outdoorsman whom Bauer trusted. So, Bauer transferred all of his company's **shares** to Niemi. Bauer used the next few years to rest and save money. By 1953, he had bought back half the shares and returned to his business. He and Niemi became partners.

In 1953, Bauer created the first US mountain-climbing **parka**. That year, American mountain climbers wore Bauer's parkas to climb K2, a famous mountain. These climbs made Bauer's parka famous, and its sales rose.

Bauer helped run the company for another decade. His son also became involved in the business. But in 1968, Bauer and Eddie Jr. sold their shares to Niemi and his son.

K2 is the second-tallest mountain in the world. It is on the border of China and Pakistan.

Three years later, the Niemis sold Eddie Bauer to General Mills. The company was bought and sold two more times after that. Today, it is owned by Golden Gate Capital. But the Eddie Bauer name remains.

BACK TO BASICS

After selling his **shares**, Bauer spent his time doing what he loved. He hunted and fished. And, he kept designing sporting goods. In fact, he developed a new fishing lure in the 1970s.

Bauer and his wife lived in Washington all their lives. They lived in Redmond and then Bellevue until their deaths. Bauer's wife died in the spring of 1986. Bauer died a few weeks later, on April 18, 1986. He was 86 years old.

Bauer improved the quality of **outerwear**. His Skyliner jacket made American sportswear better. During **World War II**, his products even saved lives.

Today, Eddie Bauer products are still known for their quality. They are also known for their style. New, more durable materials have been introduced. Colors and shapes have been updated. But Eddie Bauer's spirit, ideals, and commitment to quality have remained.

While he became a successful businessman, Bauer thought of himself as an outdoorsman first. He was happy to get back to his outdoors roots in his later years.

TIMELINE

1899

Eddie Bauer is born in Orcas Island, Washington, on October 19.

1913

Bauer starts working at Piper & Taft, a sporting goods store.

1919

Bauer opens Eddie Bauer's Tennis Shop.

1920

Bauer opens Eddie Bauer's Sport Shop.

1934

Bauer's shuttlecock design is patented. It becomes the standard in badminton.

1936

Bauer creates the Skyliner, North America's first down jacket.

1942

The Eddie Bauer company makes goods for US soldiers during World War II.

1945

The first Eddie Bauer catalog is released.

1968

Bauer sells his shares in the business.

1986

Bauer dies on April 18 at the age of 86.

GLOSSARY

caddie—a person who carries a golfer's clubs.

circulate—to move in a circle, especially to follow a repeating course.

creed—a set of beliefs or principles.

culture—the customs, arts, and tools of a nation or a people at a certain time.

down—soft, fluffy feathers.

guarantee—an agreement in which a person promises something to someone else.

hypothermia—a condition in which one's body temperature is dangerously low.

Inuit—a member of a group of native people of northern North America and Greenland.

Medieval (mee-DEE-vuhl)—of or belonging to the Middle Ages. The Middle Ages was a period in European history from about 500 CE to 1500 CE.

Olympic Peninsula—a large piece of land that sticks out from western Washington into the Pacific Ocean.

outerwear—clothing designed to be worn outdoors.

parka—a warm jacket with a hood.

racket—a type of sports equipment consisting of an oval stringed frame with a long handle that is used for games including badminton and tennis.

round—a bullet, shell, or cartridge used for a single shot.

seamstress—a woman who is skilled at sewing.

share—one of the equal parts into which the ownership of a company is divided.

shuttlecock—a small, light, cone-shaped object used in playing badminton.

symptom—a noticeable change in the normal working of the body. A symptom indicates or accompanies disease, sickness, or other malfunction.

World War II—from 1939 to 1945, fought in Europe, Asia, and Africa. Great Britain, France, the United States, the Soviet Union, and their allies were on one side. Germany, Italy, Japan, and their allies were on the other side.

WEBSITES

To learn more about First in Fashion, visit **abdobooklinks.com**. These links are routinely monitored and updated to provide the most current information available.

INDEX